FIGHTING FORCES ON THE SEA

BATTLESHIPS

LYNN M. STONE

Rourke
Publishing LLC
Vero Beach, Florida 32964

www.rourkepublishing.com

PHOTO CREDITS: title page, p. 5, 7, 8, 9, 10, 11, 17, 18, 19, 24, 26, 28, 29 courtesy Naval Institute; p. 10, 13, 15, 23, 25, 27 courtesy U.S. Department of Defense National Archives

Title page: Iowa-*class battleships matched speed and firepower. Here the Missouri* fires a six-gun salvo from her forward turrets in August, 1944.

Editor: Frank Sloan

Library of Congress Cataloging-in-Publication Data

Stone, Lynn M.
  Battleships / Lynn M. Stone.
      p. cm. -- (Fighting forces on the sea)
  Includes bibliographical references and index.
  ISBN 1-59515-461-2 (hardcover)
  1. Battleships--United States--Juvenile literature. I. Title II. Series:
Stone, Lynn M.   Fighting forces on the sea.

  V815.3.S77 2006
  623.825'2--dc22

                                        2005014714

Printed in the USA

CG/CG

Rourke Publishing

www.rourkepublishing.com – sales@rourkepublishing.com
Post Office Box 3328, Vero Beach, FL 32964

1-800-394-7055

TABLE OF CONTENTS

BATTLESHIPS

Battleships were once the most feared and famous of warships. They carried the most powerful guns and were fitted with more armor than other warships. Until the arrival of aircraft carriers, battleships were the largest of warships.

The United States Navy actively used battleships, which it designated BB, throughout World War II (1939-1945). They were used largely to bombard land targets and to fire at enemy planes attacking American aircraft carriers. The Navy scrapped or **deactivated** most of its battleships shortly after World War II. It later reactivated a few for duty in wartime.

▲

Artist Dwight Shepler shows the USS Alabama *leading American and British warships toward the Norwegian coast in 1943.*

Battleships were once the pride and focal point not only of the U.S. Navy, but also of navies around the world. Battleships were the most rugged warships afloat. They projected national pride and power wherever they traveled on the seas. America's most modern battleships, the four *Iowa-***class** ships built in the early 1940s, bristled with 9 16-inch (41-centimeter) guns that could fire 2,700-pound (1,227-kilogram) explosive shells 23 miles (37 kilometers) and more than 100 antiaircraft guns.

▲

The USS Wisconsin, *shown here in the late 1980s, is now at Hampton Roads Naval Museum, Norfolk, Virginia.*

Photographed in 1944, the USS Missouri *was one of four* Iowa-*class "fast" battleships that fought in World War II.*

The great "battlewagons" were used by several of the world's navies for decades. But as naval warfare changed dramatically with the rise of air power, battleships became increasingly **obsolete**.

Battleships were probably never quite as important militarily as they appeared. In the age before guided missiles, thundering battleship guns could inflict tremendous damage, but battleships themselves were not **invincible**. A battleship that fought toe-to-toe with another battleship could just as likely be destroyed as be the destroyer. And many smaller warships with greater speed and **maneuverability** could stay out of a battleship's range. But it was the airplane that doomed the battleship as a naval weapon of the future.

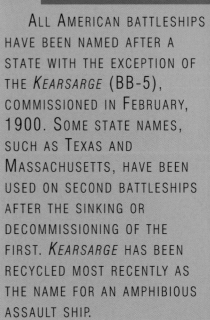

FACT FILE ★

ALL AMERICAN BATTLESHIPS HAVE BEEN NAMED AFTER A STATE WITH THE EXCEPTION OF THE *KEARSARGE* (BB-5), COMMISSIONED IN FEBRUARY, 1900. SOME STATE NAMES, SUCH AS TEXAS AND MASSACHUSETTS, HAVE BEEN USED ON SECOND BATTLESHIPS AFTER THE SINKING OR DECOMMISSIONING OF THE FIRST. *KEARSARGE* HAS BEEN RECYCLED MOST RECENTLY AS THE NAME FOR AN AMPHIBIOUS ASSAULT SHIP.

Battlewagons projected naval power for decades. Here the USS Pennsylvania *leads another battleship and three cruisers on a World War II mission in the Pacific.*

World War II proved that at least some aircraft in a large group of attacking carrier-based aircraft could avoid antiaircraft fire of battleships. They could drop torpedoes and bombs to cripple and sink battleships, then fly back to their carriers. Battleships were no match for swarms of carrier-based aircraft. Navy planners recognized that fact when they canceled the battleship USS *Kentucky* during construction in 1947. The strength of a modern naval power was not in battleships, but, rather, in aircraft carriers and **nuclear**-powered submarines.

During a span of about 50 years, the U.S. Navy built 59 battleships in 23 classes. Only 10 battleships entered service after 1923.

Battleship Specifications

Iowa Class
(In World War II)

Power Plant:
Steam turbines, 4 shafts; 212,000 shaft horsepower

Length:
887 feet (270 meters)

Beam:
108 feet (33 meters)

Displacement:
57,540 tons (52,361 metric tons) fully loaded

Speed:
33 knots (38 miles, 61 kilometers per hour)

Ship's company:
2,500-2,900

Aircraft:
2 catapults, 3 floatplanes, no hangar

Armament:
3 triple 16-inch (41-centimeter) guns, 10 dual 5-inch (13-centimeter) guns, 19 quad 40mm antiaircraft guns, 52 single 20mm antiaircraft guns

Commissioning date, first ship:
Iowa, 1943

 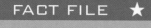
▲
On a day President Franklin D. Roosevelt described as a "day of infamy," the battleship USS Arizona, attacked by Japanese dive bombers, burned and sank at Pearl Harbor, Hawaii, on December 7, 1941.

13

CHAPTER TWO

BATTLESHIP CHARACTERISTICS

By the end of World War II, America's four *Iowa*-class battleships (*Iowa, New Jersey, Missouri, Wisconsin*) were the world's fastest and finest. Heavy with armor and guns, battleships were once considered rather sluggish at sea. The *Iowa*-class ships were anything but sluggish. The *Iowa*-class ships were the first—and the last—of the "fast" battleships. They steamed at about 33 knots per hour (38 miles, 61 kilometers per hour).

American warplanes fly over the Missouri, where Japanese leaders signed documents of surrender on September 2, 1945.

Although battleships were becoming relics of another era, a battleship at sea, from **bow** to **stern**, from deck to anchor, was still a grand picture of American naval power and class. Everything about them was big. *Iowa*-class ships were the length of nearly two and one-half full-size football fields. They had steel armor nearly 18 inches (46 centimeters) thick in some places. They had 16-inch (41-centimeter) guns mounted in three triple **turrets**. Each anchor weighed 30,000 pounds (13,600 kilograms) and each anchor chain measured 187 feet (57 meters). Bigger, better battleships were on the drawing boards and even under construction, but they would not be finished.

The Missouri's 16-inch (41-centimeter) guns fire from her forward turret in 1944. The Iowa-class American battleships were not as big as Japan's Yamato *and* Musashi, *but they were faster.*

 CHAPTER THREE

The U.S. Navy **commissioned** its first true battleship, the coal-burning USS *Texas*, in 1895. She was a large, powerful ship for her time, 309 feet (94 meters) long, protected by 12-inch (32-centimeter) steel armor, four big guns, and torpedoes.

▲
The U.S. Navy considers the USS Texas, *in service from 1895-1911, the first true American battleship.*

The mighty HMS Dreadnought *launched a new generation of modern battleships.* Dreadnought *had 10 12-inch (31-centimeter) guns and displaced 18,110 tons (16,480 metric tons).*

The USS *Kansas*, commissioned in 1907, was bigger and much better armed. But she was obsolete when she hit the water. A few months earlier, England had launched HMS *Dreadnought*. She was the first truly modern battleship. She had an improved engine, the most accurate guns yet fitted to a warship, and a top speed of 21 knots (24 miles, 39 kilometers per hour). Battleships everywhere became known as "dreadnoughts."

America's second battleship *Texas* (BB35), commissioned in 1914, is the only survivor of the World War I dreadnoughts.

America's first battleship New Jersey, *photographed in 1918 wearing her World War I camouflage paint.*

Battleships continued to grow bigger and more powerful, yet only one major battleship engagement was fought in World War I (1914-1918), the costly, but indecisive, Battle of Jutland between German and British warships. The United States did not enter World War I until 1917. American battleships saw little action beyond escort duty.

When World War I ended, the United States had the world's most powerful navy after Great Britain's. But the Washington Disarmament Conference of 1921 resulted in most countries making their navies smaller. The United States canceled seven of the nine battleships it had under construction.

Meanwhile, **foreshadowing** the future, Army General Billy Mitchell in the early 1920s had organized demonstrations to show the growing importance of aircraft to attack ships. General Mitchell's planes dropped bombs that sank old battleships. But many Navy officials did not want to accept the idea that aircraft would change traditional naval warfare.

CHAPTER FOUR

WORLD WAR II

Events of World War II revealed that the general had been right. On December 7, 1941, Japan's carrier-based aircraft sank three American battleships—the *Utah*, *Oklahoma*, and *Arizona*—and damaged five others docked at Pearl Harbor, Hawaii.

▲

USS North Carolina, *photographed on high seas in December, 1944, was a 729-foot (222-meter) long battleship that served in World War II.*

As the war progressed, several navies—the U.S. Navy was not among them—lost battleships to enemy aircraft. American planes sank Japan's *Yamato* and *Musashi*, the two largest battleships ever built, while they were at sea.

▲
Fireboats at Pearl Harbor try to put out the fire on the battleship West Virginia, *set aflame by the attack of carrier-based Japanese warplanes on December 7, 1941.*

▲

The Japanese battleship Yamato, *shown here in October, 1941, was attacked and sunk by American warplanes in April, 1945.*

Early in the war, the Battle of Midway in June, 1942, demonstrated that a major naval battle could be decided by carrier-based aircraft rather than by opposing ships shooting at each other. Wide-ranging American carrier-based planes destroyed four Japanese aircraft carriers during the Battle of Midway. Japanese carrier planes severely damaged one American carrier, the USS *Yorktown*. The warships of the two fleets never directly faced each other.

Only rarely did the big ships attack each other. At the naval Battle of Guadalcanal, battleships USS *South Dakota* and *Washington* sank the Japanese battleship *Kirishima*. At the Battle of Leyte Gulf in October, 1944, six U.S. battleships of the Seventh Fleet sank the Japanese battleship *Yamashiro*.

Warplanes, armed with torpedoes and flying from aircraft carriers, changed the nature of naval warfare during World War II.

▲
*With bowed heads, sailors aboard the battle-tested
USS* Dakota *remember shipmates who died in combat
against Japanese air attacks in June, 1944, off Guam.*

▲
A German artillery shell falls between the battleships
Texas *(background) and* Arkansas *during their
bombardment of Cherbourg, France, in June, 1944.*

▲

Aboard the USS Missouri, *a Japanese delegation arrives to sign Japan's surrender on September 2, 1945.*

Battleships also defended American aircraft carriers from attack by Japanese warplanes. It was impossible for battleships to destroy every incoming plane. But on October 25, 1942, the *South Dakota* shot down 26 Japanese aircraft to save the aircraft carrier *Enterprise*.

On September 2, 1945, Japan signed surrender documents on the deck of the battleship USS *Missouri*.

CHAPTER FIVE

After World War II, the United States rapidly downsized its battleship force. The last active battleship was retired in 1948, but the four *Iowa*-class ships were reactivated for the Korean War (1950-1953), largely to shell on-shore targets.

American battleships were deactivated again in the mid- to late-fifties. The *New Jersey* was briefly reactivated to shell North Vietnam in 1968. The *New Jersey* came back again in 1982 as a modernized missile carrier.

◀ *During the Korean War, the Missouri's 16-inch (41-centimeter) guns blasted North Korean shore targets several miles away.*

The remaining three *Iowa*-class battleships were also modernized, but the *Iowa* and *New Jersey* were taken out of service in 1991. The *Missouri* and *Wisconsin* were used during the Persian Gulf War in February, 1991, to bombard Iraqi targets in Kuwait.

The high cost of battleship maintenance and the addition to the U.S. fleet of more powerful **cruisers** and **destroyers** led to the final **decommissioning** of the *Iowa*-class ships. The last of the world's active battleships, the USS *Missouri*, was retired from service in March, 1992, ending, probably forever, the era of the great battlewagons.

Brought back again from retirement, the USS New Jersey *shelled Tuyho, on South Vietnam's central coast, in March, 1969.*

Glossary

bow (BAU) — the front part of a ship

class (KLAS) — a group of ships manufactured to the same, or very similar, specifications, such as the *Iowa* class of American battleships

commissioned (kuh MISH und) — to have been placed into official service by the U.S. Navy

cruisers (KRU zurz) — heavily armed warships, smaller than battleships, and, in recent times, armed with guided missiles

deactivated (dee AK tuh VAYT ud) — made inactive

decommissioning (DEE kuh MISH un ing) — the process of taking a naval ship out of active service

destroyers (duh STROI urz) — surface warships traditionally used to defend larger, slower ships from submarines (modern destroyers are armed with guided missiles for multi-missions)

foreshadowing (for SHAD oh ing) — hinting at things to come

invincible (in VIN suh bul) — not capable of being conquered

maneuverability (muh NYUV uh ruh BIL uh tee) — the ability to make a military or naval movement easily

nuclear (NYU klee ur) — providing atomic energy in a controlled, powerful way

obsolete (OB suh LEET) — no longer modern or of its former usefulness

stern (STURN) — the rear part of a ship

turrets (TUR utz) — armored, revolving structures on warships on which one or more guns are mounted

INDEX

FURTHER READING

Chant, Christopher. *Battleships of World War II*. Chelsea House, 1997

Green, Michael. *Battleships*. Capstone, 1998

WEBSITES TO VISIT

http://www.battleshipnc.com

http://www.chinfo.navy.mil/navpalib/ships/battleships

http://www.battleship.org

ABOUT THE AUTHOR

Lynn M. Stone is the author and photographer of many children's books. Lynn is a former teacher who travels worldwide to pursue his varied interests.